how can we find our way?

Share booklet 05

This *Share booklet* is one of a series which aims to encourage discussion about fresh expressions of church, without telling you what to do.

01 how can fresh expressions emerge?
02 how should we start?
03 what should we start?
04 how can we get support?
05 how can we find our way?
06 how can we be sustainable?
07 how can we be a great team?

Contents

Planning ahead	3
A fresh expressions journey	4
What makes you who you are?	8
Milestone reviews	10
Mission Action Plans	12
Checking the compass	14

Planning ahead

How can we find our way? is about envisaging the journey ahead by making sense of the route already travelled.

Learning through experience

This booklet does not offer you a step-by-step model but will highlight the involvement of the missional community and teams, their prayerful learning through experience and how that learning is applied in the next stage of the journey.

You will need to consider what makes you who you are, how to assess and review your progress and how to continually check that you are following God's leading and guidance.

A fresh expressions journey

Looking forward entails imagining your fresh expression's journey. One way that many ventures are likely to emerge is outlined below.

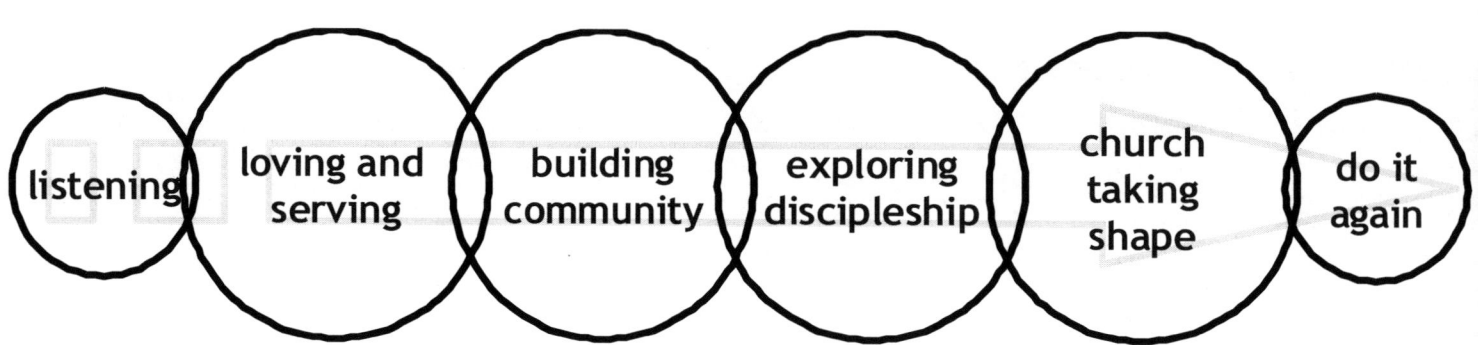

underpinned by prayer, ongoing listening and relationship with the wider church

Which way do we go?

This is a simplified description of what can be a messy process, and often the pathway will look different because of the context. It involves envisaging the next steps in your journey and asking how to travel well.

Looking to the future prayerfully is important to:

- **discern the Spirit.**

    'What pathway is the Holy Spirit laying down for us?' The kingdom comes to us from the future, like seeing through the mist the faint outline of a distant city. Out of the mist appears a runner calling with news about what the city is like, shouting out suggestions about which path to take and pointing to the help he has provided en route. Looking forward entails straining to catch the runner's words and to see where he is pointing.

- **look for the next horizon and maintain the mission focus.**

    Fresh expressions can easily plateau if they don't have a new challenge.

- **prepare adequately.**

    Practical questions may include such things as getting charitable status.

How do fresh expressions develop?
sharetheguide.org/develop

web

- **avoid pitfalls.**

    Some fresh expressions have suffered because Christians flooded into the new venture, changed the atmosphere unintentionally and reset the agenda. Looking forward can help you to avoid this and other problems.

- **build in sustainability.**

    Sustainability should be factored in from an early stage, not be something you think about later. What do you have to do now to help your fresh expression have a long life?

In the initial stages, the leadership team may ask questions like:

- **how might people experience community as the venture develops?**
- **how will the developing missional community (or team) live out its relationship with Jesus?**
- **as church begins to take shape, what might discipleship (including worship) look like?**
- **is the fresh expression starting in ways that will be sustainable?**
- **what do we have to do next?**

You won't be able to answer all these questions at the beginning. But they may help you to be intentional about the DNA you are implanting in the venture. Remember: how you begin is likely to determine the sort of fresh expression that emerges.

Later challenges may include:

- **travelling to the next stage of the journey.**
- **transitioning from the current leader to the next.**
- **how do we start another fresh expression, so that this is not just a one off?**
- **adapting to changes in context.**

Looking forward should be a continuous activity. It will help you to avoid becoming so preoccupied with 'keeping the show on the road' that you to settle into comfortable routines and things grow stale.

Looking back becomes important as the venture begins to develop. It focuses on how God has led you in recent months and over a longer period. This provides a perspective from which to look ahead.

It is a means for the Spirit to teach you through your experience. You might want to prayerfully use Sue Ballard and John Pritchard's 'pastoral cycle':

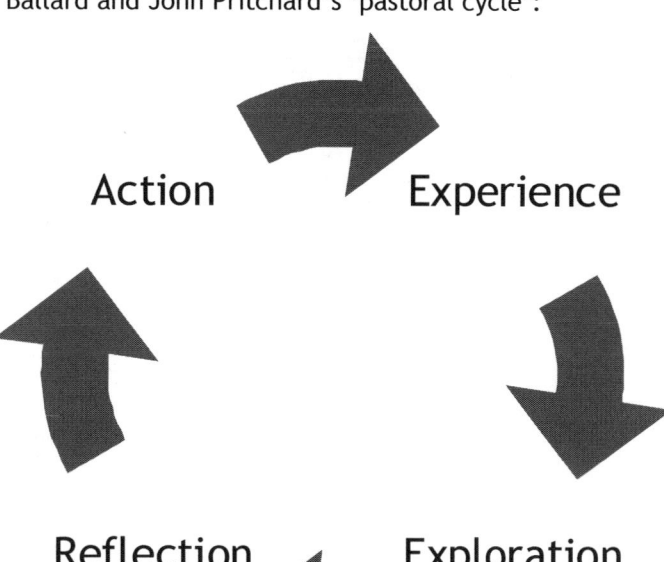

 expressions: making a difference
Fresh Expressions, 2011
Chapter 21: The Lounge at Costa

The Lounge at Costa are constantly evaluating what is working and trying new things

Experience
What have we experienced on our journey, and within the missional community? How does each of our perceptions of what we have experienced differ?

Exploration
So what's been going on? In particular, what factors have shaped our experience?

Reflection
How does God see this? What would make him thrilled? What would make him weep? What would Jesus do in the light of the journey so far?

Action
What do we need to do as a result of our exploration and reflection?

This cycle should be a continuous process. When you take action, you begin to change the situation. New dynamics come into play which you experience, explore, reflect on and act upon, and these again change the situation. Over time, you become changed.

 Sue Ballard and John Pritchard
Practical Theology in Action
SPCK, 2006, ch6

Church for the Night

Church for the Night meets at Bournemouth parish church in the heart of club land.

The aim is not to 'pounce' on any of the town's clubbers who may come in but instead offer a free café and art installation - using projections, smoke machines, light ambient dance music, and a chilled out atmosphere - to help them find space with God.

Church for the Night, held every two months in St Peter's Church from 11pm until the early hours, has featured a variety of themes, including The Friendship of God. This involved 'building' a front door and a room inside the church for people to ring the bell, go in, and answer such questions as, 'What would you say to God if he lived next door to you?'

The theme of God of the Universe was opened up through the installation of science dome housing a 360 degree cinema which mapped the stars. It also included a talk from a scientist about the cosmos. Up to 600 people came through the church that evening, mainly to sit at the front, write a prayer card, light a candle and make the most of the free cakes that Mothers' Union members had made for them.

Church for the Night is exploring what it is to be church within a different context and a different culture, looking at issues like discipleship and values - with humility, servanthood, and accountability through 'D' (discipleship) groups at its core.

The thinking also extends to how they view hospitality, giving, mission and serving one another - among other things - so that people get a real sense of what they are all about as a group and begin to build an identity without having an attitude of being 'in' or 'out'.

This experience, exploration and reflection is very much seen in Sue Ballard and John Pritchard's 'pastoral cycle'. They are now looking for the next step in the work of Church for the Night as a community which focuses on living life together, eating together, praying together, and getting involved in social action with Worship, Word, and Witness.

What makes you who you are

It is important to know the 'distinguishing marks' of your fresh expression. How does it differ from others of a similar vein and what are the values that undergird everything you do?

Values

Looking back will enable you to review the fresh expression's values. The fresh expression's values are distinctive values, specific to this particular expression of church. They are values that mark the venture out from the genre - just as the values of the Northumbrian community, for example, differ to those of the Franciscans and other intentional communities.

A fresh expression will also have 'mission values' - see  *How should we start?* (*Share* booklet 02). These are core values that could be expressed in a variety of situations. They are determined by the missional community in the very early stages, and shape its shared life and how it goes about its task as a team.

Michael Moynagh, Andy Freeman
Share: How should we start? (02)
Fresh Expressions, 2011

Sometimes fresh expressions get initial team and distinctive values confused. At the start of their work they ask, 'What values should shape this venture?' They hope for values that will be specific to the new venture, but find these difficult to discern. The venture has hardly started, so the values particular to it remain unclear.

Necessarily, values at the outset have to be rather general. They tend to be values that could apply to any number of fresh expressions. Their purpose is to guide the missional community's life and actions, and should be developed with this in mind.

Only as the fresh expression takes shape, and perhaps church within it, will the values that reflect the life of this specific body of people become apparent. They emerge in retrospect, and can be identified as part of the 'looking back' activity. They can be seen as gifts from God. They are charisms that give the emerging fresh expression its special flavour - gifts that bless its members and people outside.

In time, a fresh expression will develop:

- **initial team values;**

    These steer the missional community in its task.

- **distinctive values;**

    These mark the fresh expression out from others, the particular gifts God has given it.

    Some of the initial team values might well morph into more distinctive values as the fresh expression grows.

- **objectives;**

    These are goals that the team prayerfully sets well before distinctive values emerge.

    One goal might be that people served by the venture have opportunities to encounter Christ.

- **methods;**

    These are the means used to achieve these objectives.

    To create opportunities to encounter Christ, for example, people served by the venture can post prayer requests on to a prayer board.

- **strategy.**

    This is the overall picture, the methods being used to start and grow the fresh expression.

An example of a community's distinctive values can be found in the Potters House, Stoke on Trent. Their values are to be Spirit-filled, prayerful, creative, friendly and welcoming, young at heart, inclusive and compassionate, having high standards, culturally relevant, relational and collaborative (thepottershouse.eu/index.php?P=Who-Are-We).

Special characteristics

Remember that these distinctive values are most naturally discerned by looking back on the community's journey and asking, 'What are the special characteristics that God has given to us - things that seem to be a blessing to others and to us?'

These values may emerge gradually and take time to recognise. Perhaps periodically, as part of looking back, your missional community could ask whether any distinctive values seem to be apparent, and prayerfully compile what might be a provisional list. It might for example ask the community as a whole, and perhaps one or two people outside, whether they can identify features that make this particular venture stand out.

Over a period, it might distil these suggestions, try the list out on people and see if a consensus emerges. The aim should not be to have a long or comprehensive list, but just a few items that seem to capture what is unique to the community. A good sign might be when people say, 'Yes! That's us. That's really important!'

In smaller fresh expressions - based say in a home or workplace - it might be more difficult to distinguish between initial team and distinctive values. The first is likely to have a significant influence on the second. The important thing is to recognize and own the values you have.

Milestone reviews

Reviews are intentional opportunities to take stock and envisage the road ahead. They also offer a good context in which to look back and look forward, involving the whole community or just the leadership team.

Time to take stock

Reviews can be done informally by two friends chatting over coffee or formally as an agenda item in a team meeting. The important thing is to do them regularly and take them seriously because they:

- **build discipline into your learning.**

    Looking forward and looking back involves learning from experience and applying this learning to the future. But this learning can be uncomfortable. It may involve giving up something you thought you knew or an established pattern of thinking.

- **help you adapt to changes in the context.**

    If you don't have reviews, members of the missional community may have no forum in which to express concerns or explore new opportunities. Issues may get buried and be addressed too late.

- **enable you to manage important transitions**

    For instance, the beginnings of church within the community, the arrival of a new leader or the decision to start another fresh expression as an offshoot. Milestone reviews are a good framework in which to begin the necessary conversations.

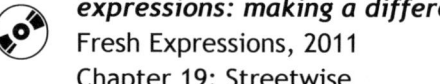 

expressions: making a difference
Fresh Expressions, 2011
Chapter 19: Streetwise

Streetwise began as a project meeting physical need, but after a review is now taking a more holistic approach.

Milestone reviews have something of a Eucharistic feel to them. They are a corporate activity, analogous to what happens at Holy Communion: the community looks back to what Jesus has done and looks forward to his return.

Milestone reviews could be undertaken within the context of an informal Communion or agape supper. This would combine worship, reflection and planning.

Dwight D. Eisenhower, the World War II general and later US President, once said:

> *Plans are worthless, but planning is everything.*
> **Dwight D. Eisenhower, Speech to the National Defense Executive Reserve Conference, 14/11/57**

The same is often true of fresh expressions.

The world is complex and fast changing, and missional communities leading fresh expressions are not in control of outside events. They have to watch out for opportunities, which may crop up unexpectedly, and seize them as they occur. In a world of flux, leadership by strategic plan should give way to leadership by discernment.

Missional communities should go with what presents rather than with what members thought was going to happen. 'Push when it moves' might be a good motto. Milestone reviews provide an opportunity to detect the Spirit's activity in a changing landscape.

Planning is indispensable because:

- **long-term planning is an opportunity for members of the missional community to have a conversation about their expectations.**

    At a later review, the community can prayerfully revise its expectations in the light of new knowledge, which then prompts further questions, 'What have we learnt? How do things look now?'

- **short-term planning is necessary for the team to know what to do next.**

    But seeing next steps from a planning-not-plans perspective allows team members to be reasonably relaxed if they have to adjust their actions in the light of circumstances. At the next milestone review, members can hold each other to account for making any changes.

Mission Action Plans

A Mission Action Plan (MAP) is one way to express the next steps, perhaps in the context of the team's longer term hopes. MAPs will vary according to the context. Larger ventures may develop quite sophisticated MAPs, while smaller ones may use something very simple. There is no one way to write a MAP.

Finding the best route

One possibility would be for your MAP to answer four questions:
- what are your plans for between now and when you next meet?
- how will you do it?
- who will do it?
- when will it be done by?

Another possibility would be to have four sections:
- a summary of your vision.
- a statement of the missional community's core values and any distinctive values that are starting to emerge.
- a short list of goals - what you hope to achieve by a specified date.
- a description of the tasks, by whom and when, to achieve these goals.

The task descriptions can form the basis of a simple statement of 'ministry expectations' for each team member (and any other volunteers), so that all are clear about what they are being asked to do and their boundaries.

Evaluation should be another part of the milestone review process. It is a way of discerning where and how the Spirit has been at work so that you can envisage how the Spirit might be leading you in future.

Measurement and target-setting has had a bad press, often because the targets are not owned by those involved. On the other hand, feedback from clients and staff is vital if you want to improve what you are doing.

A 'feedback' rather than 'target' approach to measurement can make a lot of sense within fresh expressions. Feedback can be a means of evaluating what the Holy Spirit has been doing.

Stuart P. Robinson and Mark Ireland have detailed discussion of MAPs.

Stuart P. Robinson
Starting Mission-Shaped Churches
Gospel Outreach Ministries, 2007, ch8-13

Mark Ireland
How to do Mission Action Planning. A Vision Centred Approach
SPCK, 2009

Moot

Story

The Moot monastic community offers hospitality and welcome in the City of London to 'questers' or 'spiritual seekers'. Moot members seek to deepen the ways they encounter God, themselves and others in community, spiritual formation and mission.

The community's worship draws deeply on the sacramental and contemplative traditions, aspiring to a common rhythm of life that expresses a commitment to living sustainably, holistically and justly.

In the city, Moot regularly meets people looking for resources to support their search for meaning, spiritual experience and practice. As a result Moot has been experimenting with two forms of welcome and hospitality - as part of their rhythm of life - for those resistant to traditional forms of church and evangelism.

One such welcome comes through Free Meditation sessions at Moot's 'home' in St Mary Aldermary Church, Watling Street. A group of 15 to 20 people meets every week to be led through a series of relaxation exercises into a silent meditation.

Another welcome, in a large pub in the area, sees a group meet for a 'Serum discussion' based on questions around life, God and spirituality. Starting with an icebreaker in which everyone introduces themselves, the session continues with a discussion starter and question to consider. The group then splits up into smaller groups and the ground rules of Serum are explained; the goal is not 'to win the argument' or 'get the right answer', the goal is mutual learning.

Moot has found that this approach works well, with the Christian presence and voice in the minority, because people find it much easier to listen when they no longer feel threatened by an atmosphere of dominance or control. It is not about asking people to move towards the church but instead providing a genuine space for dialogue.

Moot, through leadership by discernment, has looked out for opportunities to serve and made the most of them as they occur. They have focused on what presents itself rather than with what members thought was going to happen. Prayer continues for the discernment to recognise what may develop in future.

Checking the compass

It is all too easy to become caught up in the day-to-day workings of your fresh expression without assessing how it is going. How does it react to opportunities for growth or deal with challenges both inside and outside the church? The Spirit blows as it will - but have you set the sails to travel in His power?

How can we flow with what the Spirit is doing?

A first step would be to decide what you need to know. You might want to group your thinking around the four sets of relationships that are at the heart of church:

- **UP relationships toward God;**
- **OUT relationships in serving the world;**
- **IN relationships of fellowship within the gathering;**
- **OF relationship with the wider church (the gathering is part of the whole body).**

How well is your fresh expression growing in these four sets of relationships? To answer this you might need to identify appropriate indicators, such as the number of new people who have started to come regularly.

Charities often use quite sophisticated tools to evaluate softer outcomes - see, for example, homelessoutcomes.org.uk - and these might be adapted if you are a larger venture. Whatever you do, keep it as simple as possible.

A second step would be to decide how to collect the information. For example, you might have a discussion with a representative group from within the fresh expression, distribute a simple questionnaire or ask people outside the fresh expression (such as the head teacher in the school where you meet) about what impact they think it has had.

A third step would be to decide how you intend to use the results - for instance:

- **to inform the team's thinking, as part of milestone reviews?**
- **to aid reflection within the emerging community as a whole, perhaps through discussion during a gathering?**

These suggestions are intended to help you, and those within your missional community, to steer between no planning on the one hand and too much planning on the other. You will navigate the uncharted waters together.

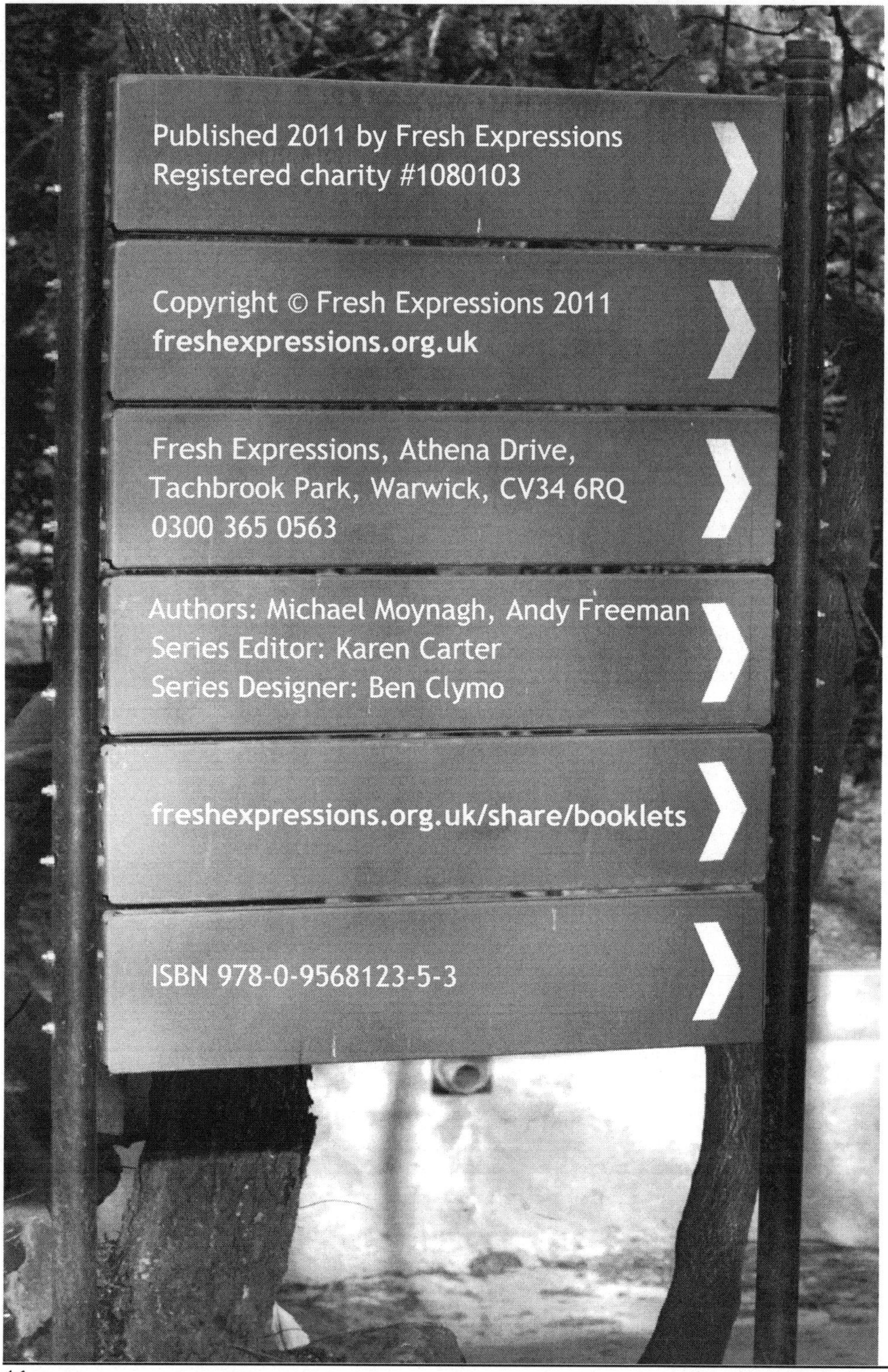

Published 2011 by Fresh Expressions
Registered charity #1080103

Copyright © Fresh Expressions 2011
freshexpressions.org.uk

Fresh Expressions, Athena Drive,
Tachbrook Park, Warwick, CV34 6RQ
0300 365 0563

Authors: Michael Moynagh, Andy Freeman
Series Editor: Karen Carter
Series Designer: Ben Clymo

freshexpressions.org.uk/share/booklets

ISBN 978-0-9568123-5-3

fresh expressions

Related resources

expressions: making a difference
(Fresh Expressions, 2011)

A DVD containing 28 stories illustrating the lessons to be learnt as fresh expressions of church make a difference to people's lives.

Available from
freshexpressions.org.uk/shop

sharetheguide.org

An online resource including a guide to fresh expressions, community, blog and learning networks.

freshexpressions.org.uk

Further stories and information, plus audio and video material and resources to download and purchase.